Another Day Someday

Tracey Odessa Kane

First published 2017
by Rowanvale Books Ltd
The Gate
Keppoch Street
Roath
Cardiff
CF24 3JW
www.rowanvalebooks.com

A CIP catalogue record for this book is available from the British Library.
ISBN: 978-1-910832-44-8

If our children are the fairy tale,
Then our grandchildren are the happy ever after.

Dedicated with all my love now, forever and
always, to Ethan, Lucy, Ezra and Arizona.
My happy ever after.

Contents

Introduction

Before you waste yet another day, think about this... There is nothing 'ordinary' about this day!

Today is a total one-off. It is unique, special, the only one of its kind, exceptional and irreplaceable in every single way. There is no amount of money that will ever, *could* ever, buy it back. There is no science, no magic, no method, no theory, no mathematical principle, no philosophy that could recreate it and recapture each and every moment of each and every life contained within it. It is priceless, and yet it has been given freely to us all.

I wonder what you will make of such a gift — indeed, what will *I* make of such a gift? Will it be wrung dry of its very greatest potential? Will its unique purpose be fully realised? Will we seize hold of the fact that this day is rare, precious, exclusive? Will we dare to boldly go where this day is desperate to lead us?

What do you think?

Perhaps we will make the same mistake as we have so many times before. Perhaps we will mix it up with all of those other days — you know, the ones where we professed that nothing much happened. The ones we saw only as 'ordinary'. The ones we wasted. The ones we wished away. The ones we regretted. The ones we ended up hating, trying to forget altogether. The ones where we simply went through the motions.

Maybe it will be missed, go unnoticed altogether, whilst we sit dreaming of that elusive creature, tenuous, ambiguous, generalised, indistinct... that Another Day, that Someday...

Hang on a minute, here comes the news flash...

Today is Another Day. Today is Someday! Today is the day for which we have been waiting, and I'm guessing the danger is that you, like so many times before, will be so busy being busy that you might just blink and miss it altogether. However, I'm hoping that you knew this Another Day, this Someday, was coming. I'm hoping you were poised, ready for it, prepared for it. I'm hoping you are expectant, motivated, energised, inspired, thrilled.

Today is a gift that time and time again we return unopened. Today is where we all too often sit and imagine what Another Day, what Someday, will be like... And yet, the truth is that today is your Another Day, your Someday...

What will you do with it?

Whatever you do, just don't blink and miss it.

Where Tomorrow Will Never Find Me

I admire and give thanks for yesterday and for all it has taught me. I look forward to tomorrow with great excitement and anticipation. But today, today has got my full undivided attention!

You see, today is the sum total of all I am, but only a reflection of who I will be. Today holds within it the stuff of dreams, the DNA of legend. Today is limitless, captivating, powerful, all-consuming, full of opportunity and possibility. Today is where I am, it's who I am, who I dreamt I would be. Today is where I prepare for who I will be tomorrow. Today is the stage on which my life is played out. Today is the book I am writing. Today is the song I am singing. Today is my ally, my closest friend, my liege. Today is my hope, my freedom, my greatest love. Today is the break I need. Today is a new beginning, a clean start, a fresh pair of eyes. Today is to boldly go where yesterday couldn't take me and where tomorrow will never find me. Today is my bird's-eye view, my white-water raft, my refuge in the eye of life's storm. Today is my window, my chance, my turn. Today is my change, my challenge, my ticket, my breakthrough. Today is my light at the end of the tunnel. Today is my signature, my mark, my goal. Today is the sum total of all I am, but not of all I will be, can be, ought to be. Today is my path made clear. Today is my star overhead, my guidebook, my map. Today is my reason, the plan, the path. Today is Another Day, Someday. Today is my happy thought. Today is my 'What If?' Today is my fresh expression, my enabler, my blank canvas. Today is my vision, my reality, my truth. Today is the first day of the rest of my life. Today is a precious gift. Today is mine. It is God Almighty's present to me, and I will open it.

Happy to Be Me

Don't look for labels to define me,
Don't read the words upon my chest,
Don't place me on the canvas that you've
painted,
Don't put me head and shoulders above the
rest.
I am not saint, nor am I wicked.
I am not black, nor am I white.
I am not big, nor am I tiny.
I am not wrong, nor am I right.
I am not a cup that's overflowing,
Nor am I a cup that sits half empty.
I am not full of wisdom and omniscient,
Nor am I irrelevant, unknowing, ignorant.
Don't look for boxes to fit me into,
And don't make assumptions on the tone of my
voice,
Don't see only what your eyes lead you to see,
And don't think I'm powerless and have no
choice.
I am not child, nor am I woman.
I am not old, nor am I brand new.
I am not special, nor am I unworthy.
I am not grey, nor am I blue.

Don't look for ways in which to portray me.
Don't rewrite my past, because it's just fine.
Don't take a scalpel to my body.
Don't give me cream to remove each line.
I am not fat, nor am I thin.
I am not rich, nor am I poor.
I am not weak, nor am I strong.
I am not certain, nor am I unsure.
I am a thousand different colours
Mixed with ten thousand different songs.
I am the wind, the rain, the sunshine,
And just like you I, too, belong.
I am the weather, ever-changing.
I am the sand. I am the sea.
I am the rhyme, so too the reason.
I am happy to be me.

What Time Will Say?

I gave you eyes to see, to open...
I gave you ears so you could hear...
I gave you a voice with which to speak...
I gave you a heart that holds life dear...
I gave you books full of great wisdom...
I gave you songs that spoke of love...
I gave you poems full of passion...
I gave you peace, so too the dove...
I gave you doctors who could heal you...
I gave you holy people who would pray...
I gave you teachers who could teach, inspire...
I gave you heroes who'd save the day...
I gave you truth and hope and beauty...
I gave you gifts to bless, to share...
I gave you talents in abundance...
I gave you emotions so you'd care...
I gave you nature, wild and gentle...
I gave you rivers, oceans, seas...
I gave you sun and moon and stars...
I gave you grass and flowers, trees...
I gave you tiny little children...
I gave you goodness, integrity...
I gave you faithfulness, compassion...
I gave you trust in what will be...

I gave you roads yet to be discovered...
I gave you adventure, risks to take...
I gave you different lands, many tongues...
I gave you culture to light your senses, to awake...
I gave you canvas upon which to paint...
I gave you colours to help you dream...
I gave you words with which to express yourself...
I gave you the answers to what life means...
I gave you deserts, forests, jungles...
I gave you mountains, valleys, hills...
I gave you seasons ever-changing...
I gave you fun and laughter, thrills...
I gave you history, timeless wonders...
I gave you stories, myths and legends too...
I gave you science and the arts...
I gave you a present each day that was new...
I gave you water with which to quench your thirst ...
I gave you food to nourish you, to help you grow...
I gave you homes to keep you safe at night...
I gave you warmth amidst the snow...
I gave you friends, I gave you family...
I gave you dads, I gave you mums...
I gave you strangers, colleagues and neighbours...
I gave you daughters, I gave you sons...
I gave you everything you ever wanted...
I gave you all you'd ever need...
I gave you all you could ever hope for...
I gave you the means to thrive, succeed...
I gave you the very best that I had to offer...
I gave you the whole world in your hands...
I gave you unending riches, all that I treasure...
I gave you a place of great honour in all my plans...
And all I ask is but one question —
Please answer truthfully, for time will tell...

What did you do with all I gave you?
Did you embrace it, did you live well?

Another Day Someday...

I've always wanted to reach, aspire
To birth the dreams inside my soul,
To live my life as was intended,
Taking risks, losing control.
I've always wanted to unearth, discover,
To travel to lands both near and far,
To taste, to hear, to see,
To follow my heart, to follow my star.
And so...
I cannot wait till Monday
To start my quest, make memories new.
You see, Tuesday was not the best time —
I had way too much to do!
I guess Wednesday was ok
But I'd already made other plans.
Oh, and Thursday was out of the question —
It's full of deadlines and demands...
Hang on...
Friday would be my best day —
But what a week it's been!
And Saturday I've planned to go shopping —
I just need a change of scene...
Don't even mention Sunday —

That day's exempt on Holy grounds!
I think I'd better stick to Monday
But not next Monday — that's out of bounds...

I've always longed for Another Day Someday
To have my time over again.
I've always wanted to boldly go,
To have the courage to catch that train...
And so...

Was It You?

Was it you who I heard singing as the sun lit up the sky?
Was it you who whispered 'good morning' as the clouds floated on by?
Was it you who told the moon to rest, for once again she had worked hard?
Was it you who folded away midnight's canvas, upon which lay many stars?

Was it you who sent the gentle breeze that carried heaven's scent?
Was it you who told the birds to sing — do you know how much that meant?
Was it you who told the flowers to open their petals and greet the day?
Was it you who woke the trees, said, 'Come on, it's time to gently sway'?

Was it you who told the butterflies to flutter near and far?
Was it you who tickled the honey bees to help them fill up every jar?
Was it you who caused the morning dew to

shine like diamonds in the sun?
Was it you who woke the fishes and told them
morning had begun?

Was it you who taught the ducks to quack and
to do that funny walk?
Was it you who told the grass to grow so we
could sit a while and talk?
Was it you who slowed time just enough for us
to stop, breathe the day in?
Was it you who wrote the book of life so each
would know where their page begins?

Was it you I saw dancing with all of the lilies in
the field?
Was it you who spread the peacock's plumes to
reveal the beauty she concealed?
Was it you who graced the morning, filled it
with joy and love so true?
Was it you who added all the richness, all the
colours, the golden hue?

Was it you who gave us hope today, gave us
faith, a reason to believe?
Was it you who showed us how to love, how to
discern your thoughts, conceive?
Was it you who taught life's heart to beat and
bless us each new day?
Was it you who gave this miraculous gift, this
present to open up today?

When Life Kicks In

When life kicks in and there's no place to hide,
Nowhere to run, your heart's open wide,
When the mirror reflects you just as you are,
Nothing very special, no rising star,
It becomes hard to focus on your visions, your dreams,
On your hopes and plans, on all your life means,
Because all you see is your faults, your chinks, your nuts and bolts,
Your flaws and the life, for some reason, you brought to a halt.
All you see are the things you got wrong,
Then you start to wonder if you even belong —
But that's when you need to stand strong,
Because the answer that you seek won't be long.
So don't be hard on yourself, start a fight!
Don't start turning your attention to night,
For all you will find there is the dark,
And demons that will tear you apart.
Don't seek solace in temptation or booze,
Don't play a game that you're sure to lose.
Believe in who you are, who you're called to be,

Not in the pale reflection others tell you they see.
Don't sell yourself short or neglect your dreams.
Don't compromise your gift, ignore what it means.
Although right now you might not believe in good,
And you would change your life in a heartbeat if you could,
Remember often we're our own enemy,
And it's we who make our own life a misery.
We all have to make choices, deal with free will —
It's just that some people are prepared to pay the bill.
And others... Well, what can I say?
They're content to simply wish their life away.

Tell Me When

When did I refuse to learn, to study?
When did I find I knew it all?
When did I tire of those around me?
When did I let my spirit fall?

For what reason did I turn away?
For what reason did joy die?
For what reason did I run, instead of stay?
For what reason must I try?

Why the need for inner peace?
Why the need for sentiment?
Why the need for hate to increase?
Why the need to circumvent?

Does anybody really care?
Does it matter if they do?
Does anybody have to glare?
Does it hurt if words are true?

Can one person make a difference?
Can one person tip the scale?
Can one person rid all hearts of difference?
Can one person make the sale?

Am I alone with all my feelings?
Am I alone and quite insane?
Am I alone with my senseless feelings?
Am I alone with my pain?

When did I stop to learn about me?
When I cease to care?
When did I become a fool for free
When I had such love to share?

Not Who But Why

There's something about standing at crossroads
That makes you move forward with care...
The road shouting the loudest invites you;
The busiest road somehow looks bleak and
bare.
But the road less travelled gets you —
It captures your mind, body, and soul!
It assures you that somehow, in your spirit,
This road is where you will become whole.
And so, pausing to take one final look down
The road which for so long you have been upon,
You reflect on all the memories you have
And you give thanks, say a prayer, move along.
Embracing this new day with passion,
Spurred on by its purpose, its call,
Understanding this is another day,
You see this is the end, so to the start of it all.
And as the road rises up now to greet you
And the sun shines in the sky, warm and true,
You get that this is your time over again
And now is about God, the universe and you!
And so you begin boldly to move forward with
courage,

With great hope and a heart full of dreams,
With the same purpose and vision,
But with a fresh revelation of what it all means.
And though the road looks narrow, looks daunting,
And friends are now few and far between,
And all you have is what's in your hand,
You understand faith and trust make a formidable team.
And as your soul finds rest, finds solace,
You learn to delight in each and every day...
Finally, the past lets you go
And the future ceases to lead you astray.
In the silence you encounter
You hear a familiar still, small voice
Willing you on, childlike, expectant,
Because this was only ever the choice.
And in your hand he places his hand
Across his face his smile lights up the sky
And in the perfect, timeless moment
You understand not who... but why.

Whilst We Lay Sleeping

Whilst everyone lay sleeping,
You helped the moon to shine,
You hung all the stars in the right spots
To show off their beauty, light divine.
You kept the whole Earth turning,
Not too fast, not too slow,
You kept the seas, the oceans ebbing,
Soothed all the sleeping giants below.
You spread hope throughout the forest
As you told of what will be,
You soothed the restless deserts,
When you gave them eyes to see.
You tenderly hushed the flowing rivers
When you sang to them love's song,
You gently calmed the crumbling mountains,
Helped them stand up, stand tall, stay strong.
You hushed the roaring wind,
Evoked in him a gentle breeze,
You stilled the raging thunderstorm,
Showed him he had no enemies.
You gave solace to the weary jungle,
Brought the smile back to her face,
You listened to the valleys grumble,

Assured her that no one could take her place.
And as all of life began to settle,
Began to rest safe in your hands,
I thought of everyone who lay sleeping,
And the parts they play in your dreams and plans.

My True Story

In the midst of life's great story
I just need some time to think,
I just need some time to ponder, because
The pages turn within a blink.
And all the thoughts that have exploded
Could be lost without a trace,
Could all be boxed, could be left wanting
Could come to naught, if not embraced.
The person that I long to be
And the book I long to write
Could be wasted, left unknown,
Without a shred of evidence, a glimmer of light.
All the hopes and dreams I treasure
All the paragraphs that make me, me
And all the mountains and the valleys
Could be erased from memory.
This is all because I did not give
A second thought, some time, a glance,
All because I did not give
My true self a fighting chance.
If I never stop and ponder,
If I never stop and think,
If I never take the time

The pages will turn within a blink.
And then how will I ever know
Who I truly am,
What I was truly made for,
Or if I really can?
How will I ever know
If each page is meant to be,
If each chapter is correct,
If this is my true story, destiny?

With Seven Little Seeds

With seven little seeds of inspiration,
And a handful of hope in what could be,
A little trust and a sprinkling of loving kindness
We could revise, change our history.
With a cup of selfless motivation
A little faith, an ounce of integrity,
A book of truth, a dish of real wisdom
We could be part of the change we want to see.
With a pocketful of courage, boldness,
And the desire to forgive, to make amends,
And with the will to love as was intended
We could live not as strangers, but as friends.

When Life Gets You Down

When life gets you down, makes you angry,
And you don't want to get out of bed,
When you feel there's no reason to sing
And you want to just dig a hole for your head...
Remember the stars up in heaven
That were put there especially for you.
Remember the moon with his glorious light
And the sun with her warmth, oh so true.
Remember the beautiful flowers
With their fragrance, their childish allure.
Remember the birds and the bees.
Remember who creation is for.

When life gets you down, makes you angry,
And you don't want to get out of bed,
When you feel like you want to give up
And you can't remember any good that's been said...
Remember the fun and the laughter.
Remember the hope that's inside.
Remember the friends that you've made.
Remember the love that won't hide.
Think of the dreams held inside you

And their place in this glorious Earth.
Think of each thought, inspiration.
Think of the price that your one life is worth.

When life gets you down, makes you angry,
And you don't want to get out of bed,
When you'd rather not look in the mirror
And you don't want to hear what's been said...
Remember the grace and the beauty.
Remember the light sent to guide.
Remember the heaven-sent peace
And the angels that ever abide.
When you start to go backwards,
And the way up ahead looks unsure,
When the darkness looks set to consume you
Just sit and be still — nothing more.

When life gets you down, makes you angry,
And you don't want to get out of bed,
When you can't think of anything nice
And you believe all the lies you've been fed...
Remember the one sent to guide you.
Remember his truth and his way.
Remember with him lie all of life's answers
And they're simply just one prayer away.

The Things I've Learned

I've learned how much our children grow
When heartache comes to call.
I've learned how much laughter helps
When your back's against the wall.
I've learned how much you value life
When the clocks tick that much louder.
I've learned how much you dare to dream
When the world is on your shoulder.
I've learned how much you treasure smiles
When heartache comes your way.
I've learned how much you see the good
When the hurt just won't go away.
I've learned how much your patience grows
When all life does is scream and shout.
I've learned how much you're thankful for
When all you see is nowt.
I've learned how much people love
When they're given half the chance.
I've learned that when all else fails
One should get up and dance.
I've learned that when things look darkest,
On hope you can depend.
I've learned that when you're frightened
God is closer than a friend.

I've learned that when you're lonely
The angels do abide.
I've learned that when you're broken
Fear has no place to hide.
I've learned that when you're empty
The truth tends to all your needs.
I've learned that when you're lost
Heaven nurtures faith's great seed.
I've learned that when there are rainclouds
Next time there will be sun.
I've learned that when I stumble
Tomorrow I will run.
I've learned that when I'm tired
I can find rest for my soul.
I've learned that when I'm ill-treated
I can still make love my goal.
I've learned, it seems, so many things
Yet I know there's so much more.
I've learned to truly value each experience
Because that, my friend, is what life is for!

Courage Is...

Courage is a summer's day that never seems to end.
Courage is telling all to a trusted, loyal friend.
Courage is an invisible rope that guides, strengthens, mends.

Courage is the promise that arcs across the sky.
Courage is the happy soul that money cannot buy.
Courage is the still small voice that says, 'Stand up! Have one last try.'

Courage is the sun that rises each and every day.
Courage is the hope that dwells in the heart and stays.
Courage is the dream resolute that will not die nor fade away.

Courage is the strength you find when all your faith seems gone.
Courage is the spirit that beckons you to run, press on.

Courage is the grace that says, 'Forgive them and fix your eyes upon...'

Courage is the truth that stands firm for all time.
Courage is the love that beats within this heart of mine.
Courage is the path we walk towards the one divine.

Mother Nature

She sleeps,
She dreams,
She keeps a close eye...
She tends,
She mends,
She doth abide by...

She nurtures,
She feeds,
She resolutely loves...
She holds,
She scolds,
She belongs to God above...

She treasures,
She shares,
She cares so much...
She imbues,
She empowers,
She adds her beautiful touch...

She amends,
She defends,

She sparkles,
She shines,
She replenishes faith... yours and mine.

She grows,
She changes,
She feels pain...

She awakens life,
She lets life sleep again...

She's courageous,
She's inspirational,
She is grace filled, true...

She is the path familiar.
She is the best of me and you.

Stop the Bells from Ringing

Decompose life's ballad,
Wipe clean the author's slate,
Pull the plug out of the ocean,
Take the mystery out of fate.

Pack away the stars, one by one,
Dampen down the sun,
Stop the children playing,
Tell the rivers not to run.

Ask the clouds to cry no more,
Make the grass shush, hold its tongue,
Flatten all the mountains,
Tell the birds to end their song.

Stop the sea from waving,
Let there be no night-time for the moon,
Return all the message bottles,
Tell the flowers not to bloom.

Stop all the bells from ringing,

Insist the wind cease to blow,
Pull up all the tent pegs,
Tell the farmers not to sow.

My true love has gone and left me,
My hopes and dreams with him he did take,
And now all life has lost its meaning...

Valentine, why did my heart you break?

The Happiness Comma

When it feels like happiness is just a comma
Between great sadness and great pain,
When your heart feels lost and lonely
And your soul can't take the strain,
Don't be bound by self-pity's bitter ropes
Nor enslaved by rejection's cruel chains,
Don't be hoodwinked by suffering's endless ways,
Don't be tempted to travel at top speed down anger's lane.

When it feels like happiness is just a comma
Between great misery and hopeless regret,
When your spirit feels crushed under the weight of it all
And you wish this life you'd never met,
Don't be tricked into thinking that pain is your lot,
Don't be fooled into believing that you have no worth,
Don't imagine that God has spat you out,
Nor that alone you shall ever roam this Earth.

For trials and test may tarry,
And happiness is often not very long,
Rest assured in the knowledge, the truth
That the happiness comma is both mighty and strong.
It will breathe life into your lungs, when you most need it,
It will inspire you, outpour hope into your soul's bank,
It will bless you with faith that will stand firm forever,
It will enable you not merely to hold on, but to thank.

So don't pitch your tent in the midst of the darkness!
Journey ever onwards with faith, hope and love as your friends,
Safe in the knowledge that after death comes resurrection
And the truth is that the happiness comma defends.

Wonderfully Magnificent

You are more than a brick in a wall,
More than tiny atoms and cells,
More than your latest mistake,
More than the story that every scar tells.

You are more than a brick in a wall,
More than you imagine someone can define,
More than a promise, a wish,
More than one moment in time.

You are more than a brick in a wall,
More than a summer that ends,
More than the sum total of parts,
More than an unfriended friend.

You are more than a brick in a wall,
More than a song or a dance,
More than a pre-painted colour,
More than an accident or a chance.

You are more than a brick in a wall,
More than a flower that blooms,
More than a bird on a wing,
More than a book that consumes.

You are more than a brick in a wall,
More than a mountaintop view,
More than a host of stars shining bright.
You are wonderfully magnificent, you!

She Is... Every Part of Me

You are the love I cannot contain,
You are the soul that I cannot control,
You are the spirit that bids me to breathe,
You are my purpose, my absolute, my whole.

You are the poet who bursts forth each new day,
You are the author who is holding the sword,
You are the wordsmith with vision and call,
You are the artist with one accord.

You are the daughter who daily obeys,
You are the infant who is learning to walk,
You are the bright, shining canvas,
You are the child who is learning to talk.

You are the cheerleader willing me on,
You are the bully trying to silence my voice,
You are the friend who betrayed me,
You are the one who said, 'You have a choice.'

You are the goodness that longs to be free,
You are the song that wants to be sung,
You are the dance that goes on and on,
You are both the right and the wrong.

You are the girl who I once knew,
You are the stranger I haven't yet met,
You are the friend I've known all my life,
You are the best of me who is still to come yet.

Beyond Our Comprehension

You cannot tame me.
I am the wind
That blows and twists and turns and bends,
That tears up your roots and fills your sails,
That from out of nowhere arrives, descends.

You cannot control me.
I am the sun
That warms and soothes and burns,
That nourishes or destroys your crops,
That your soul craves for, yearns.

You cannot own me.
I am the moon
That controls your oceans, seas,
That cuts right through your darkest hour,
That man's wildest dreams can appease.

You cannot coerce me.
I am the rain
That falls whenever and wherever I please,
That can cause a flood or even a drought,
That can bring you to your knees.

You cannot reduce me.
I am the light
That shines for all to see,
That reveals all of your darkest secrets,
That sheds the truth on hope, on history.

You cannot divide me.
I am the Earth
That has stood the test of time,
That belongs not to any mortal,
That was created by one divine.

You cannot manage me.
I am the snow
That falls without a sound,
That creates magic, beauty, a wonderland,
That takes life and buries it in stone-cold
ground.

You cannot control me.
I am the spirit
Who protects, comforts, restores,
Who guides and teaches and rebukes,
Who evens out the scores.

You cannot break me.
I am the soul
Who is and was, and will ever be,
Who creates, who writes the story,
Who defines life's great mystery.

You cannot ignore me.
I am
My hands threw stars into space,
I created every cell, every thought, every atom,
I made all that you see, the whole human race.

You cannot sell me.
I am the life
That beats within your heart,
That enables, inspires, creates you,
That makes you everything thou art.

Tell the Choir Not to Sing

Still the rising sun,
Ask the wind to hold its tongue,
Tell the birds to fly away,
For I fear there's something wrong.

Don't empty out the ashes,
Don't bake a cake today,
Don't draw back the curtains,
For my love has gone away.

Leave the church bells silent,
Put a notice on the door,
Tell the choir not to sing,
For my soul has lost her mate for sure.

No need to pick fresh flowers,
No need to pen a heartfelt letter,
No need to wrap up presents,
For this day will not get any better.

For my sweet love has gone forever,
Never to return again,
For in a cruel twist of fate,
The reaper came and called his name.

And though this day was meant to bind us,
Entwine us through vows, promises of love,
It seems that life it had a different plan,
One that I knew nothing of.

Three Words

On a crumpled piece of paper are
Three words you wrote that day,
Three words that set my heart aflame,
Three words that take my breath away,
Three words that I will cherish,
Three words that make me cry,
Three words that stole my soul,
Three words that make my spirit fly,
Three words that taste like honey,
Three words that sound like truth,
Three words that feel like silk,
Three words that offer more than proof,
Three words that say you need me,
Three words that say you do.

On a crumpled piece of paper are
Three words that say 'I love you'.
They are three words I will treasure
My whole life through.

Life

As sweet as honey to a ravenous soul,
As gentle as a breeze on a summer night's stroll,
As enchanting as a lily whose scent fills the room,
As beautiful as a rose as it's starting to bloom,
As magical as a forest lit by the sun's rays,
As inviting as blue skies on the happiest of days,
As adventurous as a baby who is learning to walk,
As free-spirited as those who love to talk,
As generous as old Mother Earth,
As priceless as any treasure you will ever unearth,
As passionate as the ocean that embraces the land,
As warm as the love that reaches out, gives a hand,
As lovely as winter, spring, summer and fall,
As blessed as the soul who sees, embraces and savours it all.

Winter's Game

I swear there'll be no summer
If winter ups his game
And carries away that one glorious moment
So it will not be seen again.

Thus all we know will be frozen,
Held in white arms that won't let go,
And everywhere we look
All we will see is snow on snow.

And all of summer's great beauty,
All her exquisiteness and charm,
Will not burst forth and bless the world
For winter will her gifts disarm.

All we will be left with is coldness
That freezes our heart and soul,
That stops us loving, learning,
Becoming healthy, becoming whole.

I swear there'll be no summer
If winter ups his game
And poor spring and her brother autumn
I fear will never be the same.

Counter Conducive

For every disaster, triumph awaits,
For every success, there's a cruel twist of fate,
For every wish granted, another dream ends,
For every enemy, the truest of friends.

For every ray of sunshine, darkness abides,
For every ounce of pain, arms are open wide,
For every regret, there's a promise of hope,
For love's every kiss, another vow is broken.

For every endeavour, there's pride and a fall,
For every nightmare, there's the greatest
surprise of all,
For every sadness, there's the gift of joy,
For every step towards peace, war will still destroy.

For every rainbow, there's a tirade of rain,
For every loss, there's a timely gain,
For every mountain, there's a valley so deep,
For every good thought, a bad one does creep.

For every misunderstanding, a truce is declared,
For every road to nowhere, a new path is shared,
For every ounce of goodness, there's tons of hate,
For every act of faith, someone leaves it to fate.

For every sad ending, a new story begins,
For every act of evil, love always wins,
For every effect, there is a cause,
For every aspect of life, there's a hidden clause.

Deliberate Choices

Be gracious in defeat
And courageous in your goals,
Undaunted by the task
And trusting in your soul.

Be faithful in all things
And joyful till the end,
Tenacious in your giving
And loyal to your friends.

Be innovative with your talents
And truthful with your heart,
Extravagant with your gifts
And frank in your desire to play your part.

Be honest in all your dealings
And bold with your hopes and dreams,
Resolute with your love
And compassionate with your schemes.

Be deliberate with your choices
And discerning with your treasures,
Protective of peace, of love, of beauty
And focused on life's author now and forever.

Are We There Yet?

Are we still here or are we there yet?
Are we halfway down the road?
Is the map enough to guide us?
Will our back really bear the load?
Will the story be exciting?
Will the breadcrumbs lead us home?
Can we stop, breathe in the beauty?
Will it be courage we have shown?
What if we end up getting lost?
What if we can't see the woods for trees?
What if it all ends up uninspiring?
What if it brings us crashing to our knees?
Should we wait until tomorrow?
Should we make a final plan?
What if tomorrow never comes?
What if this race we never ran?

Can't someone answer, soothe our tensions?
Can't someone help or give advice?
Can't someone wear this skin before us?
Can't someone just be nice?

Why must we go headfirst into learning —
Heart-first into pain,

Soul-first into misery,
Spirit-first into acid rain?

What's so great about endeavour?
What's so good about this life?
Will it be a great adventure?
Is it all just a mindless sacrifice?

Life on Life

If life sat down and reflected,
I wonder what it would think about...
What images would cross its mind?
What sentiments would scream and shout?
What would experience gently whisper?
What would reason have to say?
What would confusion be confused about?
What would empathy explain, in her own way?
How would ruthlessness defend itself?
How would lack of caring state its case?
How would intolerance fight its corner?
How would fear justify the unending chase?
What would liberty say of freedom?
What revelations would inequality share?
What truths would justice reveal?
What would love say when it took the chair?
How would the darkness justify its tactics?
How would rudeness clarify its kick?
How would self-serving explain its selfishness?
How would anger explain the fuse it lit?
What would passion get all fired up about?
What would courage say for itself?
What would hope share enthusiastically?
What would gratitude say about wealth?

What will faith bring to the table?
What will silence talk about?
What will sanctuary labour on?
What will positivity spill out?
How would failure share its lessons?
How will remorse talk of regret?
How would negativity explain its ways?
How would ignorance validate the path it set?
How would endeavour put into words and pictures
How far we've tried, but failed to come?
How will mystery and magic express, explain
All the things we've left unearthed, undone?

If life sat down and reflected,
I wonder who would command its weary soul...
I wonder who would shout the loudest.
I wonder who would try and seize control.
I wonder who would grant life room
To pause, to ponder, to take a breath.
I wonder what images would cross its mind —
Perhaps those that would leave it lost, bereft?
Or does life know things that we don't know,
And so only great possibility would it feel?
Would it reflect on time and chance?
Would it create a new and better deal?
I wonder what life would reflect upon
If it just had some time to think...
Would it be lost in awe and wonder?
Or would it see a world in chaos, on the brink?

What on Earth?

If wrath cannot be tamed,
If trust cannot be won,
If wounds can't be healed
And if once it's done, it's done,
How can we truly prosper?
How can the flowers grow?
Have we forgotten that we will reap all that we
now sow?
Will we claim to be naive and say we simply
didn't know?
What is this ignorance we foster?
Why was it left to grow?

If innocence has lost its worth,
If faith has lost the way,
If truth has lost its meaning
And if love can't save the day,
How can we say we're civilised?
There's no real evidence or clues.
There's so many hurting, violated and abused.
We cannot tolerate even one single day in
someone else's shoes.
Is it not time to look with both our heart, so too
our eyes?

Do we not see each day a little more of the plot
we lose?

If goodness cannot be tolerated,
If kindness drives us mad,
If indifference is the rule of thumb
And if we're more at ease with all that's bad,
Why do we keep insisting that we can see the
stars?
Why do we think we've got it right?
Why do we say there's no big deal, no good
fight?
Why is there apparently no need of grace, of
peace, of light?
Why do we think the death of the world grants
us life on Mars?
Why do we believe that there's no need to put
things right?

If wrath cannot be tamed,
If innocence has lost its worth,
If goodness can't be tolerated...
All I can say is, 'What on earth?'

Labels

Hell-raiser,
Trouble-maker,
Misguided,
Bore.
Ditsy,
Glitzy,
Sociable,
Whore.
Well-educated,
Silly,
Bothersome,
Insane.
Easy,
Cold,
Chilling,
Pain.
Sassy,
Classy,
Bitter,
Cruel.
Tarty,
Arty,
Sluggard,
Fool.

Insightful,
Delightful,
Pretty,
Sweet.
Unbearable,
Detestable,
Unreliable,
Neat.
Proud,
Arrogant,
Consistent,
Kind.
Willing,
Thrilling,
Merciless,
Blind.
Sleazy,
Easy,
Reckless,
Charmed.
Boxy,
Foxy,
Relentless,
Self-harmed.
Nasty,
Deceitful,
Disrespectful,
Bitch.
Genius,
Amazing,
Melodramatic,
Witch.
Inspiring,
Conspiring,
Corrupted,
Snake.
Gregarious,
Contagious,

Irritable,
Fake.
Beautiful,
Unsuitable,
Bent,
Cheap.
Lost,
Lonely,
Psycho,
Creep.
Demanding,
Angry,
Violent,
Prat.
Sexy,
Slimy,
Smelly,
Fat.
Ugly,
Waster,
Tasteless,
Vile.
Poisonous,
Callous,
Ignorant,
Wild.
Brutish,
Lame,
Man-child,
Slut.
Villain,
Hero,
Pretentious,
Butt.
Senseless,
Evil,
Charmer,
Con.

Dictator,
Anarchist,
Soldier,
Spawn.
Vivacious,
Vindictive,
Masterful,
Crackpot.
Worthless,
Endearing,
Gutless,
Swot.
Runt,
Idiot,
Liar,
Cheat.
Calm,
Collected,
Adorable,
Geek.
Willing,
Able,
Mighty,
True.
Male,
Female,
You know who!

All these are labels we see fit to use,
To lift, to crush, to con, abuse.
They're labels created to coerce, to mock, to control,
To intimidate, to flatter, to abuse, to console.

All these are labels that define this life,
Used to make others lesser, to cause them strife.
They're labels that cause joy and pain in equal measure,

That blind us, bruise us, enslave and tether.

All these are labels that dictate all the rules,
Saying who is acceptable, who is not cool.
They're labels that bring suffering, division,
That separate us through lack of love, of vision.

Labels will speed us towards our end
Labels can kill, destroying neighbour and friend.

Stranger Danger

Do you fear my
Brokenness,
Like I fear
Yours?
Do I make you
Feel uncomfortable,
Like I have
A hidden clause?
Do I put
A strain upon
Your heart,
Your mind,
Your soul?
Do I leave
Your spirit
Wanting?
Do you think
Causing you
More pain
Is my end goal?
Do I remind you
Of the ghosts
That roam
Inside

Your head?
Do I make
You feel
Afraid?
Do I make
You wish
You were
Dead?
Do I
Intimidate
Or offend
You?
Does my
Very presence
Grate?
Do you despise
All that I am?
Am I a cruel
Twist of fate?
Because a
Mirror
Never
Lies...
But it also
Sees the
Truth
Quite plainly;
The one I fear the most
Looks an awful
Lot like...
Me!

Not So Civilised

We love to feed the ducks
Whilst children starve to death —
It sounds loveless, sounds absurd
And yet there's no deep intake of breath.
We love to wash our cars
Whilst children die of thirst —
It sounds far-fetched, unbelievable,
And yet the truth is it gets much worse.
We love to save our every penny
Whilst children make our clothes —
It sounds ridiculous, insane
And yet what no one sees, no one knows.
We love to buy our homes
Whilst children live out on the street —
It sounds mind-bending, cold and cruel,
And yet we all but tread on them under our
feet.
We love to wear the latest fashion
Whilst children are bare and left exposed —
It sounds heartless, abhorrent,
And yet this epidemic grows and grows.
We love to proclaim our achievements and
education
Whilst children have no books, no school —

It sounds unenlightened, detrimental,
And yet we think that they're the fool.
We love to have all the latest gadgets
Whilst children have never seen a toy —
It sounds heart-breaking, devastating,
And yet never real kindness do we deploy.
We love to drive the latest model
Whilst children have no shoes on their feet —
It sounds merciless, disgusting,
And yet with finest leather we cover each seat.
We love to live life like we matter
Whilst children daily die lost and alone —
It sounds insidious, appalling,
And yet we act like we've never seen or known!

Sister, My Sister

Sister, my sister,
Don't hang low your head —
Look up, stand tall, raise your voice!
Don't fear that man, all he has said —
Equality is your birthright, not his choice.

Sister, my sister,
Don't hide your light —
Let it shine, let it light up the world!
Don't let that man keep you hidden, enslaved —
Freedom is your birthright, not his dark
underworld.

Sister, my sister,
Don't banish your dreams —
Set them free, see, believe, watch them grow!
Don't listen to that man who claims you have
no value —
To dream, to conceive is your birthright, not his
to blow.

Sister, my sister,
Don't punish yourself —
You are precious, you are beautiful, wise and kind!

Don't let that man cause you to cut, hurt
yourself —
Justice is your birthright, not his to corrupt,
undermine.

Sister, my sister,
Don't you sell your soul,
Hold tight to all that you will be, that you are,
Do not give up, give in, to that man and his
schemes,
Your soul is your birthright, not his to pull down,
to mar.

Sister, my sister,
Don't box up your heart —
Let it beat, let it love, let it breathe!
Don't let that man kill and destroy, tear it apart —
Your heart is your birthright, not his to crush,
deceive.

Sister, my sister,
Don't grieve your spirit —
Set her free that she might seize, run her race!
Don't let that man trip you up, keep you down —
Your spirit is your birthright, not his to misplace.

Sister, my sister,
Please don't end your life —
For soon a brand new day will dawn!
Don't let that man strip your meaning away —
Life is your birthright, not his to use as a pawn.

Sister, my sister,
Don't hang low your head —
Look up, stand tall, raise your voice!
Don't fear that man and all he has said —
Equality is your birthright, not his choice.

A World Without Sanctuary

Go home... you don't belong here.
Go home... look, read the signs.
Go home... there's no place for you.
Go home... what's mine is mine.

Get out... you are not welcome.
Get out... there is no room.
Get out... these things are *my* things.
Get out... don't just turn up and presume.

Go back... to where you came from.
Go back... take your family too.
Go back... to your own country.
Go back... we don't want the likes of you.

Stop taking all our resources.
Stop stealing all our jobs.
Stop filling all our houses.
Stop trying to even the odds.

Of course we are all of the good people.

Of course we are polite.
Of course we are well-educated.
Of course we understand your plight.

But our country is... well, you've said it — it's
our country,
And I'm afraid that we must make it clear
That of all the places in this big, wide world,
You will find no sanctuary here!

Of course we will set up charities to help you,
And we will sing songs to honour our endeavour,
But the truth, quite plain and simple, is...
You can't put your roots down here — not ever!

Like poison, our evil words drip off our tongues,
Clogging up hearts and souls and minds...
Like acid rain they kill, destroy all that is decent
and good,
Leaving only bitterness, ignorance and
intolerance behind...
Until all we see are enemies and strangers,
Until all we do is fear and hate,
Until our world becomes ever more inhospitable,
Until even hell closes its gates.

The Richest Man in Bolton

I met a man with no shoes.
His soul was laid wide open, bare.
He cared not for fashion
And he didn't wish for a comfy chair.
He was full of wit and wonder.
He embraced life like a child.
He drank beauty in like water
And a list of his treasures, he had compiled.
He loved the colours in a rainbow
And he loved the clouds up in the sky.
He loved the busyness of life
As it quickly hurried by.
He loved the sound of children's laughter;
He loved seeing their eyes sparkle, shine.
He loved the smell of coffee
And he thought roses were divine.
He loved the sound of silence.
He loved each drop of rain.
He loved the stars at night
And he loved dusk turning to day again.
He loved the kindness of strangers;
He loved each helping hand.
He loved to be there just to listen.
He loved those footprints in the sand.

He loved the sound of music
And he loved to watch people dance.
He loved to sing his heart out.
He loved to reminisce about his childhood in France.
He loved the wisdom of the elderly
And he loved the effervescence of the young.
He loved both courage and compassion.
He loved chocolate — how it melted on his tongue.
He loved life's wonders and its mysteries, indeed,
He loved life through and through!
And I am so blessed that I have met him,
The man who has no shoes.

Write the Future

When the past finally
Catches up to the present
And the future smiles,
Tips its hat...
When the song in the air
Grows louder
And all of your hopes and dreams
Are still intact...
When the road that's before you
Beckons
And the stars sparkle and shine,
Lighting the way...
When the spirit inside
Cannot be contained,
For it knows what
The good book does say...

Time and chance
Come together
When we've forgotten
That hurt we once knew...
When we've said sorry,
Let go of our anger...
When we've forgiven

The ones who hurt you
And when no more
You let fear dictate things...
When you let go,
Stop trying to control,
And you come out of
The shadows...
When you let grace
Restore, heal your soul...

At once everything
Starts to look different.
The past
No longer stings, overwhelms,
And the present
Looks quite pleasant
After all.
The gifts and the talents
You buried for so long
Now begin to come into their all
As the past catches up to the present.

As the future smiles, nods its head,
You remember all that God promised,
And you give thanks for
The book that you've read.
You pick up your pen
To write the future,
Capturing every word
That life's author has said.

Testament

If you freely give respect,
If you resolutely share your peace,
And extravagantly employ your gifts,
You'll see your happiness increase.

If you care with joy and kindness
If you have hope in your heart,
If you have faith in your who, your why
And you're prepared to play your part.
If you freely share all that you have,
If you love unconditionally,
And you strive to be the change
To be the best you can be,
Then yours will be a blessed life
Full of beauty, passion and grace,
Yours will be a life well lived,
A testament to the human race.

The Poet and the Muse

Sometimes I don't know
Who will turn up to write...
The poet? The teacher? The activist?
Always right — always ready to fight.

Perhaps it will be
The dreamer? The brave? The child?
The down-hearted? The untamed? The wild?
The rich? The poor? The angry? The insane?
The bully? The victim? The bold? The tame?
The healer? The leader? The physician? The
clown?
The loyal friend who's always around?
The educated? The civil? The dead?
The mysterious? The aloof? The terribly well-
read?
The adventurous? The loaf minus a slice?
The peaceful soul? The one holding a knife?
The life coach? The cheerleader? The fool?
The lost? The lonely? The uber-cool?
The entrepreneur? The investor? The cad?
The angel? The saint? The super-bad?
The inconsistent? The embittered? The freak?

The one who asks too many questions? The one
who likes to retreat?
The woman? The daughter? The mother? The
girl?
The one slowly letting her wings unfurl?
The zealot? The crazy? The black and white?
The politician who's always right?
The entertainer? The youth?
The frail one? The bulletproof?
The dominant male? The misunderstood?
The cheeky one, always up to no good?
The elderly? The frail?
The one who too close to the wind does sail?
The head of the dog,
Or the wagging tail?
The poet and the muse... the poet and the muse.

Bright and Glorious

On the hour, every hour
Strength born out of pain,
Courage crushed yet undefeated
So it picks up the sword and writes again.
For there is a truth that must be told
A tale that all must hear,
And neither darkness nor hatred
Should silence the sword, cause it to fear.
For trickery and cruel deceit
May serve the demons well,
But heed that looming change!
Heed that tolling bell!
For love has started growing —
She gains new followers every day,
And light and hope and passion
Now all their parts will play.
So fret not throughout the winter,
For spring promises new life will be born,
And that new life will yet lead us all
To a bright and glorious new morn.

My Kind of Beautiful

You are my kind of beautiful,
My kind of magic, mystery.
You are the colours of my rainbow
And you are by far the best of me.
You are a tenacious, unending melody
That fills my spirit with passion, with happiness.
You are the full stop that completes me
And you are the reason that I am blessed.
You are my summer sunshine
And you are my meadow of wild flowers.
You are my every granted wish
And you are the dream that fills my hours.
You are the very air I breathe
And you are my dearest friend.
You are the light within my soul
And you are the dance that never ends.
You are the greatest love of my life
And you are the wind beneath my wings.
You are my kind of beautiful
And you are the reason that my heart sings.

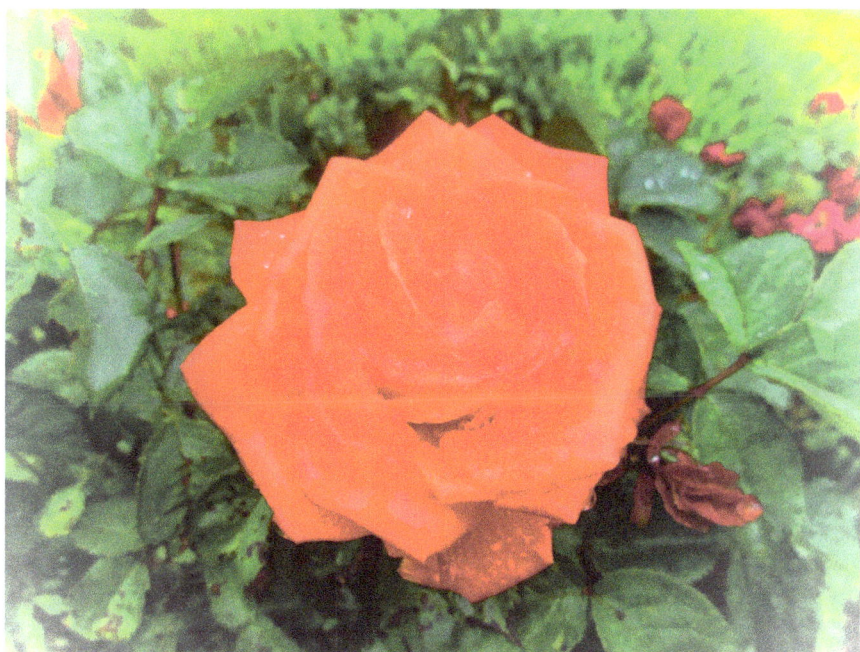

The Measure of Love

Love can't be measured by the hours in a day,
Nor can it be measured on a scale.
It cannot be quantified by the width or in miles.
It cannot be bought or sold, or purchased in a
sale.

Love can't be measured by the rays of the sun,
Nor can it be affected by the moon.
It cannot be found at the end of rainbows.
You cannot tell it where or when to bloom.

Love cannot be measured by the droplets of the
sea,
Nor can it be boxed and stored away.
It cannot be tempted, can't be coerced.
It cannot be washed away by rainy day.

Love cannot be measured with a plumb line,
Nor can it be counted by the sands of time.
It cannot be tamed or be controlled.
It cannot be forced to be sublime.

Love cannot be measured by the stars in the sky,

Nor by the countless waves upon the shore.
It cannot be stored up or be buried.
It has to love as it is loved and nothing more.

Summer Wine

He watches with joy and reverie
As the singing birds wake up the morn.
Hid behind piles of dusty books,
His glasses sit quite forlorn.
Though the room is silent
His thoughts jump like gazelles,
Running to and fro within his mind,
Touting tickets for memories held.
Diving, always diving,
Searching, dipping deep,
Unravelling life's DNA
And waking up that which is fast asleep.
Swimming as if in an ocean,
His memories, hopes and dreams combine,
Until he catches, quite by chance,
The one that tastes of summer wine.

The Shirt Off Your Back

When you've said all you have to say
And you've listened with an open heart,
When you've weighed up the truth before you
And you've made room for healing to start,
Don't regret the past or what has been!
Don't seek ways to rewrite the story!
Focus on the lesson life is teaching,
Not on your desire to grab some glory.

Allow purpose to explain there's no need to try
To be whiter than white — you're not perfect;
Indeed, to be perfect is not part of your why!
Life is for living; it's not created to be but a project.
You are here and you're on your own journey —
There's no destination, no kudos, no medal,
No clock to punch, no copy to publish,
No agenda, nothing feigned nor instrumental.

Trial and error will be the day's order
As you live, as you breathe, as you dream,
As you chart your way through life's forest,
As you discover what it all really means.
So have courage, have faith in life's author!

Don't try to be all things to all men!
Don't punish yourself when you fall.
Don't be afraid to stop, turn around and try
again.

Embrace both the good and the bad.
Learn from the young and the old.
Dance as often as you are able
And don't believe everything you are told.
Love like there is no tomorrow,
Like there's no danger you'll ever be hurt.
Love the friend, the foe and the stranger
And from off your back give them your shirt.

Not One Ounce

If I speak in colours,
If I see a song,
If I hear a touch,
Do I truly not belong?
If I think in silence,
If I walk and never run,
If I treasure all that's good,
Would you say I had blinkers on?
If I feel things with my head,
If I have wisdom in my heart,
If I listen to what's unspoken,
Does that mean I play no part?
If I believe in angels,
If I write and paint and sing,
If I speak to God,
Are my gifts useless, unfit to bring?
If I perceive each miracle,
If I understand the truth,
If I love as I am loved,
Do I not need to show you proof?
It seems you have a checklist
Of all you think I should fulfil;
It seems you're ill at ease

Because I'm willing to pay life's bill.
It seems that you don't trust me —
Indeed, I don't think you trust anyone at all —
And that may be your real problem:
You have not one ounce of trust in life at all.

One Day of Freedom

Don't look into my future
As if it is your past,
And don't hold me accountable for your dreams
If they were never built to last.

Don't chain me to your endeavours
If they lack justice, equality,
And don't try and bind me in your contract
If it means I lose my freedom and liberty.

Don't seek to rule over
My family or my life,
And don't say I asked for it
Like some ball-and-chain you labelled 'wife'.

Don't speak for me, bear witness
If your language is cruel, crass,
And don't claim to stand up for my rights
Then ban me from walking on your grass.

Don't act all high and mighty
Like you've got things oh so right,
And don't act like judge and jury
Like you think you've won some fight.

Don't say that you have my back
When a knife's clutched in your hand,
And don't label me valueless, insane
Just because you fail to understand.

Don't label me as foolish
Because I would not play your game,
And don't assume I acted in haste
Because I jumped off your so-called gravy train.

Don't think I won't amount to much
If you are not around,
And don't think I'll be lost and lonely
Hidden deep underground.

Don't think that you are stronger
Because I choose with kindness, grace,
And don't label me inferior
Because I will not run your race.

Don't laugh at me or mock me
Because you think I'm weak, frail,
And don't spit your dummy out
Because I've left your shores, set sail.

Don't think that I don't love you,
Because that simply is not true!
What I did, I did for the greater good,
For a world I long to share with you.

Something More Inside

Don't be afraid to start again —
There's always something more inside,
Something yet to be discovered, unearthed
Something not yet perceived, not yet breathing,
alive.

Don't be afraid to start again —
They've not yet played the final song,
And there's still time to reach, to aspire,
Still time to dream, have courage and be strong.

Don't be afraid to start again —
There's still time to write that book,
So many things to learn, to question,
So many roads to choose, paths that we
overlook.

Don't be afraid to start again —
There are more hats for you to wear,
More adventures, more sights to see,
More people to love, more people who care.

Don't be afraid to start again —
There are more rainbows, more pots of gold,

So many wonders, so many memories,
So many beautiful things to experience and
behold.

Don't be afraid to start again —
There's always something more inside,
So much more than you dared hope for, or
imagined,
So much to make, to thank God that once more
you tried.

A Beautiful Truth

A beautiful truth,
A ballad sublime,
A kiss from a rose,
A moment in time...
A whispering willow,
A dream taking flight,
A glorious someday,
A perfect delight...
A hug sent from heaven,
A treasure lost and found,
A bolt of inspiration,
A welcoming sound...
A beautiful sunset,
A heartfelt desire,
A love for all seasons,
A faith that won't tire...
A blessed adventure,
A song your heart sings,
A life-changing encounter,
A passion that wins...
A beautiful truth,
A ballad sublime,
A most extravagant present,
A life freely given, divine...

The Original Dream

There is no plan B, no plan C or plan D.
There is no other hope than me, than you.
There is no alternative answer.
There is no hidden clause, no clue.

The original dream is all that there is,
Born out of a love for the world, for mankind.
The original dream, called plan A,
Is the only blueprint you will ever find.
For the path was clear; the way was so pure...
Such a magnificent masterpiece to behold!
Its foundation was built on the firmest of
ground,
Crammed full of treasures and wisdom of old.
So much potential... it left you breathless.
So much to unearth... such depths to seek!
So many wonders beyond all measure
And so many tongues with which to speak.

But then into this glorious picture
Come two hands, two feet, a man,
And in his lack of grace, of wisdom
He made a fire with the original plan.
And slowly, bit by bit, he changed things

Until no more of the original dream was left,
He rewrote the rules, culled all of life's goodness
And left Mother Earth in despair, bereft.
He lost sight of life's true riches,
Preferring instead manmade dross.
He crippled life with such endeavour,
He thought that he was good, that he was the boss.
He thought that he had all the answers.
He thought that his way was the best.
He cared not for natural order;
Wanted life to bow, to kneel at his request.
He did such a job on love and mercy
That they left us long, long ago.
He ridiculed peace, freedom and justice.
He left hate and intolerance to grow and grow.

And now...

We all wait in empty vessels
For our number to be called,
Oblivious to how things could have been,
Blind behind our manmade walls.
There was no plan B, no plan C, or plan D.
There was no other hope on Earth,
We missed the point of plan A, the original dream
And of all it was truly worth.

Life's Greatest Call

When into the darkest night I roam
Remind me of that fire at home,
For 'tis the solace of that place
That bade me rise and run my race.
For though I buckle,
Though I despair,
I do not yield to comfort's chair;
I say a prayer and take my leave,
And the promise of peace I do perceive.
If I am to help make it so,
I need to face both friend and foe,
For all are needed to make the change
To tip the scale, to rearrange.
All are needed to fight the good fight,
To shine love's light into darkest night.
All are needed to make amends,
To rewrite the story before it ends.
All are needed, one and all,
To answer this, life's greatest call…
To love as you are loved…
To love as you are loved.

Wake Up... It Is Time

Brother, won't you carry me,
Lift my weary soul,
Tend me with a mother's love
Heal me and make me whole?
For long has been my journey
And treacherous my path,
And empty were my pockets —
The sum of nothing do I have.
Yet still I travelled onwards,
And held firm to the belief
That when I found my brother
He'd offer me relief.
And so stars by night I followed,
The sun by day did guide,
And the trials and tests along the way
Freed my soul from indifference and pride.
And the silence spoke to me daily
Of life, of love, of place,
Of sanctuary and sanctity,
For the whole of life, the human race.
The wind spoke of his great hope
That one day we would learn,
That for everyone there is a place
And for everyone there is a turn.

And the wilderness, she shared her own heart;
She explained her many fears.
She spoke of how mankind has lost its way
And how each of us sits alone in tears.
Still she was not discouraged;
Like the wind, she had great hope,
For she believed with all her heart and soul
That mankind would learn to do so much more
than cope.
And the forest echoed these sentiments,
For he too saw mankind's good;
He knew that the day would come
When mankind would see things as they should.
He firmly believed that change was coming,
That the call had been sent out,
That mankind was slowly waking;
Their light was slowly but surely inching out.
Although the creatures still feared their thirst
for blood
And their sheer lack of grace, control,
They too saw mankind's potential
And understood they'd lost their way, their soul.
Both the day and night agreed
That life could be made complete, be restored,
With lots of love, care and kindness
And with everyone on board.
The rain had the final word;
She said, 'All things have their time...
We must all be courageous, strong and patient!
We must protect the plan divine!
Soon we'll see a brighter dawn
When light and love and joy abound,
When balance is redressed
And when truth, humility is found.'
She added, 'Until then, I must travel onwards
And find my brothers and sisters,
Souls who are awakening,
Who are prepared to do what they must do.'

And so I started walking,
Relearning all the wisdom my spirit once knew...
I hoped against all odds I'd make it home —
I was desperate to reconnect with you.
And so, brother, now I have found you,
I ask you will you carry, help to share my load.
Will you join me on the path I walk
And use once more all you have and hold?
Will you help me to wake our family
As it sleeps in want and waste?
Will you help me teach and inspire
Others to join us, to run their race?

Brother, oh my brother,
Do you hear me? Do you care?
Will you lift my weary soul?
Will you help me give back to life, make it fair?
Brother, oh my brother,
Can you hear this heart of mine?
It's calling out to you,
Saying, 'My brother, wake up! It is time.'

Author Profile

Tracey Odessa Kane's lifelong passion, writing, emerged during her childhood. The youngest child in a forbidding family situation, writing became her most trusted ally, her saviour; it gave her solace and allowed her to think and to say all those things that her everyday life wouldn't allow her to voice. Her experience of being a young mother had a profound influence on her and her writing. Having always dreamt of writing books that could help people like her who had been forced to suffer imposed silence, she seized the motivation she'd gained from having a son. She wanted above all for people to know they were not alone, that they were loved, valued, had worth and purpose, in spite of the hand life may have initially dealt them. And so Kane's quest began. For the past thirty years, she has dedicated her life to helping those whom for whatever reason cannot help themselves. She's volunteered to help her Church and community, and has worked within charity and education sectors. Her desire to help others to communicate has always played a huge part in this, so much so that she has received awards both locally and nationally. Although she left school at a young age with no qualifications, she loves to learn and has furthered her education, forming links with not only Sheffield and Chester University, but with a wide and varied range of training providers, including The Institute of Leadership and Management and The Coaching Academy. It is Kane's belief that everyone matters and has the absolute right not only to be heard, but to be educated, equipped, empowered and encouraged, to be treated justly with fairness and equality, and it is to this cause that she dedicates her life and her writing.

Publisher Information

Rowanvale Books provides publishing services to independent authors, writers and poets all over the globe. We deliver a personal, honest and efficient service that allows authors to see their work published, while remaining in control of the process and retaining their creativity. By making publishing services available to authors in a cost-effective and ethical way, we at Rowanvale Books hope to ensure that the local, national and international community benefits from a steady stream of good quality literature.

For more information about us, our authors or our publications, please get in touch.

www.rowanvalebooks.com
info@rowanvalebooks.com

Rowanvale
Books

www.ingramcontent.com/pod-product-compliance
Lightning Source LLC
Chambersburg PA
CBHW042339040426
42448CB00019B/3336

Publisher Information

Rowanvale Books provides publishing services to independent authors, writers and poets all over the globe. We deliver a personal, honest and efficient service that allows authors to see their work published, while remaining in control of the process and retaining their creativity. By making publishing services available to authors in a cost-effective and ethical way, we at Rowanvale Books hope to ensure that the local, national and international community benefits from a steady stream of good quality literature.

For more information about us, our authors or our publications, please get in touch.

www.rowanvalebooks.com
info@rowanvalebooks.com

Rowanvale
Books

www.ingramcontent.com
Lightning Source LLC
Chambersburg PA
CBHW042339040426
42448CB00019B